ULTIMATE MAPPING GUIDE FOR KIDS

By real-life explorer
Justin Miles

First published in the UK
by QED Publishing
Part of The Quarto Group
The Old Brewery
6 Blundell Street
London N7 9BH

ISBN 978-1-78493-464-4

Author: Justin Miles
Publisher: Maxime
Bouknooghe
Art director: Susi Martin
Editorial Director:
Laura Knowles
Production: Nikki Ingram

Designed, edited and
picture researched by
Tall Tree Ltd
Editor: Joe Fullman
Designer: Jonathan Vipond

Printed and bound in China

10 9 8 7 6 5 4 3 2 1
15 16 17 18 19 20

CONTENTS

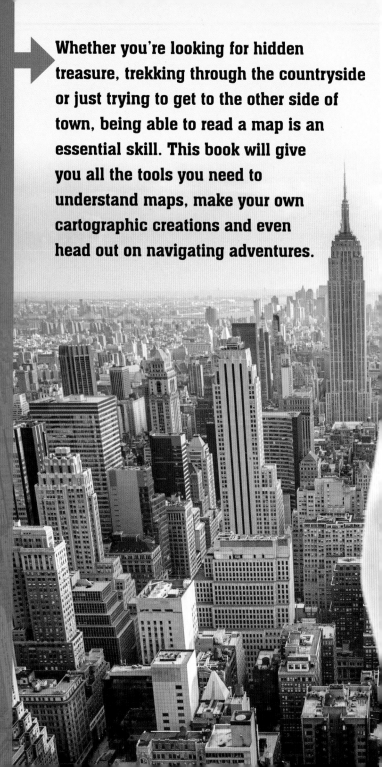

Whether you're looking for hidden treasure, trekking through the countryside or just trying to get to the other side of town, being able to read a map is an essential skill. This book will give you all the tools you need to understand maps, make your own cartographic creations and even head out on navigating adventures.

These days, incredibly detailed, interactive maps are available at the touch of a button on computers, mobile phones and other electronic devices.

USING MAPS

There are many different types of map. Some show an area's physical features while others give detailed information about routes. This chapter will introduce some of the most common types.

First things first: what exactly is a map? A map is a drawing or picture of a place, a country or even the whole world as if seen from high up, like in a hot-air balloon, on a plane or even from space!

COMMON MAP TYPES

Physical maps, like this one of India, use colours to highlight an area's natural features, such as mountains, deserts, forests and rivers. **They are also often shaded to look three-dimensional and to show the different heights of the land.**

Road maps are flat plans that show streets and roads to help drivers, cyclists and pedestrians find their way around, but they don't show hills, mountains, or valleys. **Road maps also show important or useful buildings and landmarks, such as hospitals and car parks.**

Topological maps only show the basic information of where places are on a route. They are so simple that they look like diagrams. **Public transport systems are often shown as topological maps, such as this map of the underground network, or 'Tube', in London, UK.**

Grid line

Contour line

TOPOGRAPHIC
MAPS

Topographic maps give a detailed view of what's on the ground, including buildings, rivers, forests and fields. These maps also show the height and steepness of hills and mountains by using lines called contours (see pp.32–33). Most topographic maps have lots of symbols (see pp.18–19) and are covered in grid lines which make it easy to pinpoint locations (see pp.26–27).

Because they give so much detail, people use topographic maps to navigate in the countryside.

TYPES OF MAP

The first maps were etched on pieces of stone around 14,000 years ago, while the earliest portable maps were made on clay tablets. Modern cartographers use the latest computer and satellite technology to make sure their maps are as accurate as possible.

SATELLITE
MAPS

Many modern maps are made using detailed images of the Earth taken by satellites. One of the great things about satellite maps is that, if you're looking at them on a computer, you can pan out to see an entire country or zoom right in to see a close-up of your street.

NORTH AND SOUTH

On most maps 'North' is at the top of the page. But this is just because we are used to thinking about the world this way – which is why this map looks strange. But it isn't actually wrong. There isn't really an 'up' or a 'down' in the universe!

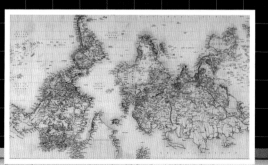

POLITICAL MAPS

Political maps show the boundaries between official areas, such as countries and states, counties and towns. Like this map of North America, they often use colours so it's easy to tell the different areas apart.

CHANGING
THROUGH TIME

If you look at old maps of your home town, you can see how it has changed and evolved through history. Can you find out if your home was on a map 50 or 100 years ago?

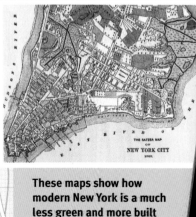

These maps show how modern New York is a much less green and more built up place than it was in 1767.

The most accurate map of the Earth is a globe because it shows the planet's actual spherical shape. In order to turn a globe into a flat map, cartographers have to slightly distort the shapes of the countries. This is known as making a projection.

ENCIRCLING THE GLOBE

Lines of latitude and longitude form an imaginary grid covering the Earth, which can be used to pinpoint locations on its surface.

Lines of latitude run horizontally around the Earth, dividing it into a series of slices. Lines of latitude don't touch.

Lines of longitude run vertically around the world. Unlike lines of latitude, longitude lines meet at the North and South Poles. They divide the Earth into a series of wedge shapes.

The Equator is the line of 0° latitude. It runs around the middle of the Earth at its thickest point. All global positions are measured as being north or south of this line.

The Prime Meridian is the line of 0° longitude from which all directions east or west are measured.

The Equator

Lines of longitude

MAKING A PROJECTION

Turning a spherical globe into a flat map is a bit like peeling the skin off of an orange. Once the surface has been flattened down, there will be gaps between parts of the world. Map-makers have to stretch these parts to get them to join up. Over the centuries, they have come up with several different ways of doing this. You can see two different projections here.

Note how the size and shape of the countries are slightly different in each of the maps.

Prime meridian

Lines of latitude

TOP TIP

Lines of latitude and longitude are spaced out at regular intervals and are measured in units called degrees, written °.

You can make your own maps of all sorts of places, from your desk to your neighbourhood. Here are some steps you can follow to get started.

MAP OF YOUR OWN DESK

Start small, by making a map of your desk.

1. Lean over your desk or table so that you can see everything on it.

3. Label the different objects on your 'desk map'.

2. Draw the outline of the table first, and then draw each object. Remember that you're drawing the shape of the object as you look straight down on it. Try to think about where the objects are in relation to one another and how far apart they are.

Sailors use nautical maps of the seas and coastlines called charts.

MAP OF YOUR
HOME

Making a map of your house or garden is a real challenge.

Use grid paper and make each square equal to a set length, such as 20 cm, in real life.

Measure the walls, furniture and doors, and the distances between them.

Carefully draw everything onto your paper, using a ruler for the straight lines.

MAP OF YOUR
NEIGHBOURHOOD

Try making a map of your neighbourhood – from memory.

1. Imagine walking around your neighbourhood. Picture it in your mind.

2. Draw the streets and write down their names. Estimate how long they are.

3. Mark where you think your house, your friends' houses, and any other buildings you know, such as schools, restaurants, or shops, are.

4. Now compare it to a real map of your area. How did you do?

If a map isn't available, it's still possible to find out where to go by asking someone for directions. But you need to remember what you've been told, so that you don't get lost.

When giving directions, imagine walking the route in your mind.

MAKING
WORD MAPS

When giving directions, people usually try to paint a picture with words. This is known as making a 'word map'. Read the word map for this picture – which gives directions for how to get from the house with the blue pointer to the house with the red pointer – and then try to come up with one of your own.

3. 'Turn right in front of the green house, and walk down the road.'

2. 'Turn left and head past three large houses on the right.'

1. 'Turn right out of the house and walk up the road until you get to a crossroads.'

TOP TIP

Try making your own compass rose on a piece of paper using a pair of compasses and a pencil. Place it on the floor and then tell your friends which direction to walk in to find something that you've hidden.

COMPASS ROSE

A compass rose is a design on a compass or map showing the four main directions: north, east, south and west. These are also known as 'cardinal points'.

N

Cardinal points

NW

NE

W

E

SW

SE

S

Intermediaries

In between these cardinal points are more directions know as intermediaries: north-east, south-east, south-west and north-west.

In between the intermediaries are even more points, as shown by these white lines.

4. 'It's the fifth house on the right, opposite the house with the red roof.'

IN THE OPEN

In an open space, such as a park, you could guide people using features such as trees or ponds. But in a a wilderness area, you would probably have to give directions using compass points.

A map's legend contains all of the information that you need to read your map correctly. The legend is sometimes also called the key.

SYMBOLS

Rather than write the names of all a map's features out in full, which would take up a lot of space, map-makers use symbols instead. Symbols are little pictures of the places they are supposed to represent. The meaning of each symbol is written in the map's legend.

Airport	✈	Train station	
Hospital	✚	Bus station	
Museum	🏛	Cafe	
Shop	🛒	Restaurant	🍴
Petrol station	⛽	Police station	
Post office	✉	School	
Main road		Minor road	
River		Park	

Check the legend on the left to find out what these symbols mean.

WARNING

Keep Up To Date!

Roads and paths can be moved, buildings can be demolished, and areas of forest cut down, so the more up-to-date your map is, the more accurate it will be. Always take a recent map with you.

GO THE
DISTANCE

We can fit towns, cities and even whole countries on a single piece of paper. When looking at a map, how can we work out how big the real place is, or how far we have to travel? It's all about scale.

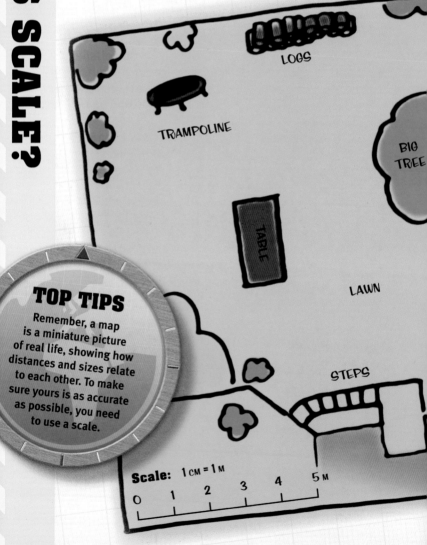

WHAT IS SCALE?

When you create a map, you have to draw everything much smaller than it is in real life so it can fit on the paper. Everything must be reduced by the same amount, so all the features stay in proportion. This amount is known as the scale.

LOGS

TRAMPOLINE

BIG TREE

TABLE

LAWN

STEPS

TOP TIPS

Remember, a map is a miniature picture of real life, showing how distances and sizes relate to each other. To make sure yours is as accurate as possible, you need to use a scale.

Scale: 1 cm = 1 m

0   1   2   3   4   5 m

USING SCALES

Scales differ from map to map.

For instance, if you were making a map of your garden, like this one, you might decide on a scale where one metre in real life is shown on your map as one centimetre.

To make sure everyone understands what you've done, you could write your scale on the map as:

$$1 \text{ cm} = 1 \text{ m}$$

Or you could draw a scale bar on the map, like this, so people can tell at a glance what the distances on the map are supposed to be:

0　1　2　3　4　5 m

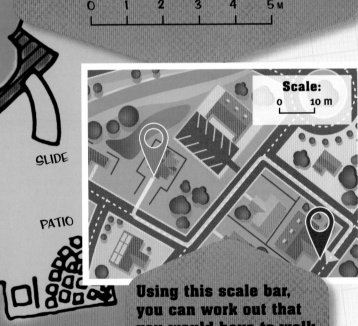

SLIDE

PATIO

HOUSE

Scale:
0　　10 m

Using this scale bar, you can work out that you would have to walk for 95 m to get from the house with the blue pointer to the one with the red pointer.

Maps are drawn to many different scales. A map of your town would have a totally different scale than a map of the whole world drawn on the same sized piece of paper!

LARGE, MEDIUM AND SMALL

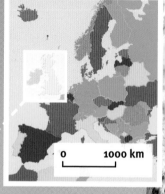

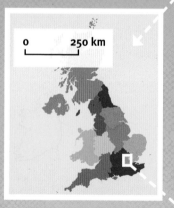

A small-scale map actually shows a very large area, such as the continent of Europe (above).

A medium-scale map shows a slightly smaller area, such as a country.

A large-scale map shows a small area, such as this one of the centre of the city of London. The larger the scale of the map, the more detail that can be shown on it.

The scale for each map is shown by the scale bar.

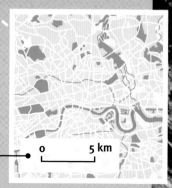

CREATE YOUR OWN
SCALE MAP

Here's a challenge:
draw a map of your
garden to scale.

1 **Use a tape measure** to
measure the size
of your garden and everything in it. If you don't
have a garden, you could make a map of a room in
your home instead.

2 **Now you can draw a map** using a scale of five
centimetres on the map to one metre in real life –
or whatever scale you choose.

3 **If you don't have a tape measure**, you
could measure your garden in paces and create
your own scale.

SCALES AS FRACTIONS

**Another way of showing the scale on a map
is to use a 'representative fraction'.**

A scale of one centimetre to one kilometre could
be shown as either: 1:100,000 or $\dfrac{1}{100,000}$

This shows that one centimetre on the map
represents one kilometre in real life because
there are 100,000 centimetres in a kilometre.

To find the distance between two points,
measure it on a map with a ruler and then use
the scale to calculate the distance in real life.

WHAT'S THE POINT OF GRIDS?

Most maps are covered in a grid of horizontal and vertical lines that divide the map into equal-sized squares. You can use this grid both to find and to describe where things are on a map.

GRID REFERENCES

The position of each square can be identified by its grid reference. This is a combination of numbers (and sometimes letters) running along the bottom and up the sides of the map. These numbers are known as easterlies and northerlies.

1 **When giving a grid reference, first give the easterlies** – the horizontal line of numbers, reading left to right.

2 **Then give the northerlies** – the vertical line reading from the bottom up.

3 **Give the reference for where the lines cross** in the bottom left-hand corner of the square you want.

25

24

23

22

Northerlies

The grid reference for this square would be written as:
1221

21

11 Easterlies ● 12 13

The squares on the grid usually fit with the scale of the map. For instance, on a 1:100,000 scale map, each square on the map represents one square kilometre in real life. This makes it fairly easy to calculate distances.

Scale:

0   1 km

TOP TIP

Some maps use only single numbers, while others use a combination of numbers for the easterlies, and letters for the northerlies. Go to p.77 to see what a map that uses both numbers and letters looks like.

GRIDS
WITHIN GRIDS

The six-figure grid reference for this location would be written as:
128212

10
9
8
7
6
5
4
3
2
1

1 2 3 4 5 6 7 8 9 10

Grid squares on a map can be quite big and cover a large area.

To show the exact position of something within a grid square, you could use a six-figure grid reference.

Imagine a grid of horizontal and vertical lines within each main square of your map grid, with ten lines running in each direction – a grid within a grid.

Each line has its own number, from 1 to 10, running left to right for the easterlies, and bottom to top for the northerlies, just like on the main grid.

Give the grid reference in this order: main easterly, inner easterly, main northerly, inner northerly.

CLIMBING HIGH

As everyone knows, the world isn't flat. It's a sphere with an uneven surface of low and high areas. But maps are created in 2D on flat paper. How can we show what the land is really like?

Ever since the first maps were made, people have been trying to work out the best way to show the difference between areas of high and low land.

Jagged mountains can be tricky to map accurately.

SIDE-ON VIEWS

On very old maps, hills, mountains and valleys were drawn as if seen from the side. Mountain ranges were shown as a collection of peaks. This wasn't a very accurate method because it didn't show the true height of the mountains.

Pointy symbols like these are not a very clear way of depicting mountains.

LAYER TINTING

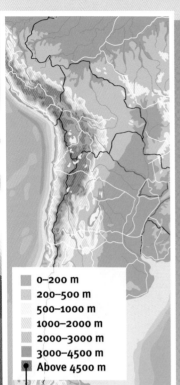

0–200 m
200–500 m
500–1000 m
1000–2000 m
2000–3000 m
3000–4500 m
Above 4500 m

This key shows the height above sea level represented by each colour and shade.

As map-making developed, cartographers started showing heights using a special technique called layer tinting.

This uses colours to match approximate heights so that you can see areas of high and low land and where mountain ranges are.

Have a go at making your own map using layer tinting. Draw an imaginary island with a high mountain range, some lower hilly areas, and a wide, flat area. Then fill in a key to show the height of all these areas.

WARNING ⚠

Rough Guide

Maps that use layer tinting can only give a rough guide to an area. As they don't show the shape and steepness of the hills, mountains and valleys, they shouldn't be used by travellers planning a route.

The most accurate way to show the height, depth, gradient (steepness) and shape of an area of land on a map is by using contour lines.

Hill shown by contours.

807

Areas of forest can also be shown using tree symbols and green shading.

HIGH
AND LOW

Contour lines link up areas of the same height. Lines that are wide apart show a gentle slope, while lines that are close together indicate a steep incline.

CONTOUR SHAPES

Contour lines can show you the shape of the land as well as its height. This can help you to recognise where you are, and plan a route. By studying the shape of the land, you can avoid steep hills, valleys and cliffs, and look for easier paths.

A pattern of ring-shaped contour lines tells you that the the feature is...

...a cone-shaped mountain.

821
810
800
790

Where contour lines actually touch or overlap, there is a cliff.

Sometimes a stone will mark the highest point on a mountain.

SPOT HEIGHTS

Black dots are used to show high points, such as the top of hills or mountains, with the height written alongside in numbers. These are called spot heights.

760

750

740

730

The height of each line is written in a small break in the lines.

TOP TIPS

When you're looking at a contour map of a mountain range, you can sometimes find a 'pass', which is the lowest point between the mountains where there might be a river, a road or a footpath you can follow.

08
800
810
820

A pattern of contour lines like this shows that the feature is...

...a range of four sharp peaks.

Here's a quick way to make your own, one-of-a-kind contour map.

MAKE YOUR OWN CONTOUR MAP

Place rock in water 1

Carefully place the rock in the middle of your bucket and add just enough water to cover the bottom.

5

Pour a little more water into the bucket so it reaches the first level on your scale. Then draw another chalk line around your rock at the height of the water and copy that onto your paper to make your second contour line.

Repeat all the way to the top to finish your map.

Draw the remaining contours

770

YOU WILL NEED

- A large rock or irregularly shaped object
- A bucket big enough to put the rock in
- A jug of water
- A piece of chalk
- Paper, pencil

2

Mark 'sea level'

Using the chalk, draw a line all the way around your rock at the level of the water. This is your 'sea level'.

Draw a scale

Use the chalk to draw a scale on the side of your bucket, such as 1 cm to 100 m, 2 cm to 200 m and so on.

3

Look down at your rock from directly above and draw the shape of the first chalk line onto your paper. This is your first contour.

Draw a contour

4

Cartographers don't just map areas of land. Since the mid 20th century, they have also been making maps of the sea floor.

This map of one of the deepest parts of the Pacific Ocean shows a side-on view of undersea mountains. Colours have been added to the image to show the height of the mountains.

BATHYMETRIC MAPS

A map that shows the physical features of land on the surface is called a topographic map. Its undersea equivalent is a bathymetric map.

Did you know

Maps of the sea floor are used by scientists studying underwater habitats, by treasure hunters on the look out for sunken ships, and by the world's navies to help them safely guide their submarines.

Sonar device
Original wave
Reflected wave
Deep valley
High peak

HOW TO MAP THE SEA FLOOR

Most of the sea floor is hidden from view, so how can cartographers make maps of it?

In ancient times, sailors dangled heavy ropes off the sides of their ships to find out the sea's depth. Today, cartographers use sonar devices, which send sound waves down to the sea floor. By measuring the amount of time it takes for the sound waves to bounce back up to the device, it is possible to work out the shape and depth of the undersea terrain.

GRADIENTS

The angle, or steepness, of a slope is known as its gradient. This is shown in the form of two related numbers. The first is the vertical distance, the second the horizontal distance. For instance, on a 1:10 slope, you would climb up 1 m for every 10 m you went forward.

1:10 A gentle slope

1:5 A medium slope

1:1 A steep slope

GOING
OUTDOORS

Exploring the great outdoors is fantastic fun. But it's even more fun if you have the right equipment, follow simple safety rules and treat the countryside with care and respect.

First things first – don't go out on a mapping mission into the wilderness without the right gear.

Make sure your rucksack is adjustable and comfortable to wear.

FOOD AND DRINK

Always carry plenty of drinking water in a reusable plastic bottle or hydration bag. When you're out exploring, you'll get hungry, so make sure you take meals or high-energy snacks depending on how long you plan on being out.

Hydration bag

Energy bar

CORRECT CLOTHES

Wearing the wrong clothes and shoes is the quickest route to a navigation nightmare.

- Make sure your walking boots or shoes fit properly. Ill-fitting boots can cause blisters.

- Dress according to the conditions and remember to 'layer up' if the weather is cold.

- Always take a hat! A hat can keep your head warm, keep the sun off your face and neck, and keep you dry.

TOP TIP

Even if it looks like it's going to be a warm, bright, sunny day, always pack a waterproof coat. Conditions in the countryside can change unexpectedly and very quickly. Don't get caught unprepared!

KIT TIPS

Rucksack Large enough to carry all you need.

Compass Learn to use it.

Watch It's easy to lose track of time, but if you take a watch, you'll know when to head home.

Mobile phone Your lifeline – be sure to put it in a waterproof bag.

Camera To remember the day.

A mapping adventure can be great fun, and is usually absolutely safe, but sometimes accidents happen. Follow these safety rules to make sure a great day out doesn't turn into a disaster.

If you walk on ice and it breaks, you'll be plunged into freezing water.

WARNING

Stay Away!

⚠ Never go near water, rivers or lakes without an adult with you.

⚠ Frozen lakes and rivers are really dangerous, even if the ice looks thick. Never try to walk on the ice.

⚠ Never explore farmyards, abandoned buildings or construction sites.

ALWAYS CARRY...

There are certain items you should always carry with you, particularly if you're going to be far from civilization.

First aid kit With plasters, bandages and antiseptic wipes.

Small wind-up torch

Emergency whistle

Waterproof matches Never use matches without an adult being present.

Thin plastic poncho In case of bad weather.

Penknife With blades and other useful tools – again, use only with adult supervision.

Foil blanket

Pencil and paper

LET THEM KNOW

Always make sure that you have your parents' permission before you go out. Tell them where you'll be, who you'll be with, and what time you'll be home. Once you've planned your route and told your parents, don't change it without telling them first.

When learning to explore, it's a great idea to take an adult with you – so you can stay safe together.

It's great to explore the outdoors, but it's important that you look after the countryside so that it's there for everyone to enjoy.

DOING THE RIGHT THING

There are rules in the countryside, just like in towns and cities.

All land is owned by someone, so make sure you have permission to explore before you do.

Follow any signs and keep to marked footpaths when you're crossing open land.

If you need to open a gate, make sure you shut it behind you. If a gate is already open, leave it open.

ANIMAL SENSE

If you have a dog with you, make sure you keep it on a lead at all times. Never try to feed or play with wild or farm animals.

Stay away from farm animals, especially ones with sharp horns!

Always be sure to leave gates as you found them when crossing farmland.

TOP TIP

• Don't drop litter and make sure that anything you take with you, you take home again.

• As the saying goes, 'Take nothing but photographs and leave nothing but footprints'.

WARNING

Cause no harm

 Don't damage any hedges, plants or trees.

Always walk around the edge of fields so that you don't harm the crops.

Never light fires. Wildfires can destroy vast areas of land, kill birds and animals, and risk human lives.

NAVIGATION

Navigation is the art of getting from one place to another. Most of us rely on memory to guide us around in our everyday lives. But what if you're going somewhere new?

Many advances in navigation have been made by sailors. The first ocean navigators would stay within sight of the coast and use landmarks to help them find their way.

Modern sailors rely on satellite technology to guide them.

FINDING THE WAY

Early sailors used things like wind direction and measuring the water depth to help them navigate.

As navigation developed, sailors would use a big, heavy tool called a cross-staff to measure the angle between the horizon and either the Sun or a star. That angle would tell them how far up or down the globe they were (their degree of latitude). The cross-staff was replaced by a smaller, simpler tool, called the sextant, which ocean navigators still use today.

An antique brass sextant.

LONGITUDE

To calculate how far east or west they were (their longitude), sailors had to know the local time and the exact time on the prime meridian. That was impossible until the British clockmaker John Harrison invented an accurate seagoing clock, or chronometer, in 1764.

The Earth rotates through 360 degrees over 24 hours, which is 15 degrees per hour. So, by knowing the difference between the local time and the time at the prime meridian, sailors could finally calculate their exact degree of longitude.

An 18th-century marine chronometer.

MODERN NAVIGATION

Identifying their position using latitude and longitude allowed sailors to make pretty accurate maps from the 18th century onwards. Modern maps of land, coastlines and seas use satellite imaging and are almost 100 per cent accurate.

Satellites have mapped the Earth in great detail.

People use numerous tools to help them navigate. You'll already be familiar with some of them.

MAPS AND CHARTS

People exploring the wilderness use topographic maps. These show as much detail as possible about the height and shape of the land, as well as all of its geographical features.

Detail of an ocean chart.

Waterproof map cases, such as this antique one, keep your maps dry and in good condition.

People navigating the oceans or waterways use special maps called charts.

TOP TIPS

Both simple and advanced technologies have their uses. Always carry a pencil and paper for noting down useful information. Remember, the functions of many navigation tools can be performed by smartphone apps.

NAVIGATION KIT

These are some of the most useful pieces of equipment for guiding you around and telling you where you are.

Orienteering compass
Shows you Magnetic North, and has direction lines which can be used to plot your course on a map.

GPS unit
Its satellite technology can both tell you where you are and allow your family and friends to follow your journey online.

Pedometer Measures how many steps you take. If you know what direction you walked in, you can use it to figure out where you are.

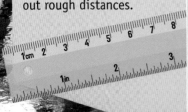

Altimeter Shows you how high you are above sea level. You can use that information with the contour lines on your map to find out where you are.

Ruler If more advanced technology isn't available, you can use a ruler and your map's scale to work out rough distances.

Map measurer A small device for measuring distances that aren't in a straight line. Just wheel the measurer along your route and the reading will tell you how far it is.

Since its invention around 1,000 years ago, the navigating compass has proved an invaluable tool for sending people in the right direction. But how does it work?

Compass needle

A magnetic compass consists of a tiny magnetic bar, called a compass needle, balanced on a small pivot, which allows it to spin around. Like all magnets, the compass needle is attracted to other magnets.

The Earth has a metal core, which makes it act like a giant bar magnet, creating a magnetic field around the entire planet.

MAKE YOUR OWN COMPASS

Magnetise needle

1
Turn a needle into a magnet by holding it in one hand and stroking it with a magnet. After about 30 strokes your needle should be magnetised!

2 Float needle
Cut a small disc of cork and place it so it's floating in the middle of a bowl of water. Lay your needle carefully on top of it so it's right in the centre.

The needle will turn until it eventually points north!

North

Find north! 3

The compass needle spins around to point to the top of the Earth's magnetic field – otherwise known as Magnetic North. No matter where you are on Earth, your compass needle will always point north.

Just to confuse you when you're out navigating with a map, there are three 'norths' to think about!

This giant compass rose in Lisbon, Portugal, points to True North.

THE FIRST NORTH!

Lines meet up at the North Pole.

The first 'north' points towards the geographic North Pole, the spot at the top of the Earth where where all the lines of longitude meet. The direction of the lines of longitude is known as True North.

THE SECOND NORTH!

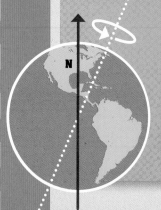

The next 'north' points to the Magnetic North Pole. The pole is created by the Earth's magnetic field. Because the Earth is on a slight tilt, the magnetic field doesn't align with the geographic North Pole. Magnetic changes in the Earth's core mean that the position of Magnetic North is constantly moving.

When exploring by boat, the Vikings released birds from cages. If the birds came straight back, they knew land wasn't near, but if the birds flew away, they followed them to find land.

Did you know ?

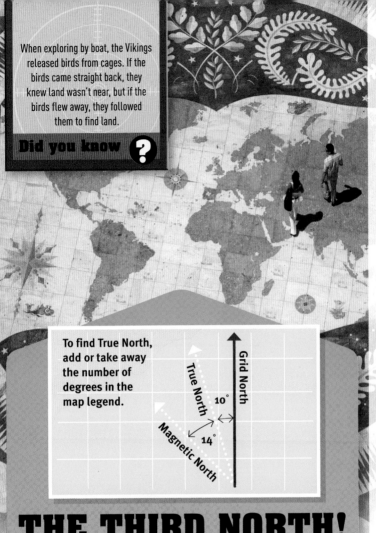

To find True North, add or take away the number of degrees in the map legend.

Grid North

True North

Magnetic North

10°

14°

THE THIRD NORTH!

The last 'north' is Grid North. This is created by the grid system overlaid onto your map. Although a map is flat, the area it covers is actually slightly curved because the Earth is a sphere. This makes the straight north–south grid lines on a map slightly inaccurate.

In the legend of most maps you will find a diagram showing the degree of difference between the three 'norths'. Knowing the difference will help you to navigate accurately. The difference is called variance or declination.

Sometimes it's helpful to orient, or line up, your map so that it is facing the same way that you are. There are three main ways of doing this.

BY SIGHT

To orient your map by sight, first look in the distance to find three features that stand out. These features could be a high mountain, a building or a lake. Put your map on the ground and find the three features on it that you've chosen. Turn your map until you can trace imaginary lines to your chosen features.

You are here

When you've done this, your map will line up with what you can see – and you've oriented your map!

LINING IN

Use this technique to find out where you are on a map.

Look as far into the distance as you can to find a prominent feature and identify it on your map.

Then you need to find another feature about halfway between you and your first chosen feature. On your map, draw a line from the farthest feature through your second feature and on towards where you think you may be standing.

you are here

Repeat the exercise with two more features. Where all your drawn lines cross, that's your location!

USE A COMPASS

Lay your map on the ground. Turn the dial of your compass so that north on your compass wheel lines up with the index pointer. Put your compass on your map with the orienting lines running the same way as the north–south lines on your grid.

Turn your map and compass together until the orienting arrow lines up with the north end of your compass needle. You and your map will now both be facing north.

The compass parts are explained on p.59.

Navigating with a map and a compass is a very useful skill and is really easy to learn.

HOW TO USE A COMPASS

Mark points **1**

Lay your map out flat on a level surface. Mark your start and finish points on the map.

Finish

Start

Place compass **2**

Place your compass on the map with the long straight edge of your compass base plate leading from where you are to your destination.

Hold the compass in your hand with the direction of travel arrow pointing away from you. Turn your body so that north (N) on your compass lines up with the red orienting arrow. The direction of travel arrow is pointing the

7 pick a point

When you get to your marker, repeat the exercise.

Pick a point – a visible marker in the distance – and walk towards it.

6 Direction of travel

COMPASS PARTS

Base plate

Direction of travel arrow

Orienting arrow

Index pointer

Orienting lines

Dial

Magnetic compass needle

Rotate dial **3**

Rotate the dial to line up the orienting lines with the lines running north and south on the map. Make sure that the red orienting arrow is pointing north on the map.

The number on the dial that lines up with your direction of travel arrow is your compass bearing. Note it down.

4 Bearing

Bearing of 270° shown here.

Variance

Don't forget to add on or take away the number of degrees to account for the variance between the grid on your map and your compass!

5

A compass bearing is simply the angle of the line you need to walk along to get from your starting point to where you want to be. But what if you can't see your destination? That's when taking an intermediary comes in handy.

Intermediary

USING
INTERMEDIARIES
. . . .

Use your compass to take a new bearing.

Sometimes the feature that you're walking towards on your bearing may be a long way away or may become difficult to see once you get into thick woods or hilly country. This is when you should use an intermediary.

An intermediary is something you can see that's in a straight line between where you are now and where you want to be.

Take a bearing using the intermediary and use it to move towards your destination.

When you reach the intermediary, take another bearing, either of your destination or, if that is still obscured, another intermediary.

TOP TIPS

Each time you take a new bearing, make sure you write it down in your notebook so that you will be able to retrace your steps if you get lost.

Destination

Direction of travel

When you're taking a bearing, you need to ensure that the compass is totally level so that the needle can swing freely.

GET YOUR BEARINGS

Remember, every time you turn to walk on a different angle, you need to take a new bearing.

When you take your compass bearing, pick a fixed feature in the distance.

BACK BEARING

If you want to double-check your direction, you can take what it is known as a 'back bearing'. This means reconfirming your position by locating yourself against three prominent features, just as as you would do when you first orient your map (see pp.56–57).

Pick the three most prominent features you can see.

Orienteering is a map-reading sport that can help you to improve your navigational skills.

HOW TO ORIENTEER

Orienteering is a sort of fast-paced map-reading race. Competitors navigate around a course using a topographic map.

On the way, they must find a series of set points using compass bearings or grid references given to them by the race organisers. Whoever completes the course in the fastest time is the winner.

A temporary flag, which can be moved to a new position for each race. The code is hidden inside.

At each set point there is a marker or flag with a number or letter code. Competitors must record the code to prove they have found it.

Most orienteering races are staged in the countryside, where you really have to know how to read a map.

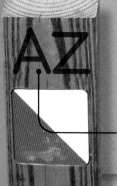

A permanent orienteering post marked with a letter code.

INDOOR ORIENTEERING

You can play an orienteering game indoors!

1 **Write a number on five sticky notes** and hide them around the room.

31   12   4

21   55

2 **Put a marker in the middle of the room**, such as a piece of paper stuck to the floor, so you know where the start point is. From that marker, use a compass to write down a bearing for each sticky note.

3 **Give a compass and a list of the bearings to each competitor.** The race is then on for them to find all the notes and write down their numbers.

You can play the same game on a larger outdoor scale in your school playground, in your garden or at the park. The game works in exactly the same way, with hidden markers, a marked start point and a list of compass bearings.

The compass bearings for both games can be given either from the start point or from one marker to the next.

NAVIGATING*
(*WITHOUT A COMPASS!)

Sometimes you may find yourself away from home and want to know which way to go. But what do you do if you haven't got a compass or if your compass is broken?

If you find yourself out in the wilderness in the Northern Hemisphere without a compass, all is not lost. There are still ways to find out where you need to go.

At noon in the Northern Hemisphere the Sun is always directly south. Stand with your back to the Sun and you will be facing north. Your right arm will point east and your left arm will point west. Simple!

TRACKING THE SUN

The Sun rises in the east and sets in the west, making it easy to work out north and south at those times. To find these out at other times, you will need a stick, a watch, some string and a couple of small stones.

1 **Put the stick in the ground** (the taller the better) and mark where the tip of its shadow falls on the ground with one of the stones.

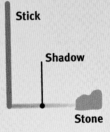

Stick

Shadow

Stone

2 **Wait 20 minutes.** The shadow will have moved. Mark its tip again with the other stone.

3 **Mark a straight line** between the first stone and the second using the string. This is the west–east line. The first stone is pointing west, while the second is pointing east.

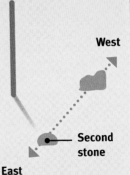

West

Second stone

East

USING A WATCH AS A COMPASS

To tell what direction you're facing when it's not midday, you'll need a watch with an hour and minute hands. Make sure it's set to the right time.

Sun

1 **Lay the watch on a flat horizontal surface**, such as a table or your hand.

2 **Turn the watch so that the hour hand is pointing at the Sun.** Draw an imaginary line between the hour hand and the 12 o'clock mark on the dial – that is the north–south line.

South

North

3 **If you're in the Southern Hemisphere,** point the 12 o'clock mark at the Sun. Then draw an imaginary line between the 12 o'clock mark and the hour hand to get your north–south line.

South

North

TOP TIPS

In the Northern Hemisphere, look for patterns of moss growth. The northerly, more shady sides of trees and rocks will generally have more moss growing on them than the southern sides.

Even when it's dark, you can still use the stars in the night sky to work out which direction you should be heading in.

STAR COMPASS

You can find out all four compass points, just by lying on your front. For this technique, you'll need two long sticks.

1 **Lie down on the ground** in the direction of a bright star.

2 **Push one of the sticks into the ground**, so that its top is at eye level.

3 **Push the other stick into the ground in front of the first stick** so that its top lines up with the star.

4 **Now sit and watch the star** for a few minutes. Note which direction it moves from the top of the second stick.

- If it moves upwards, you are facing east
- If it moves downwards, you are facing west
- If it moves right, you are facing south
- If it moves left, you are facing north

Try to keep still while star-watching

THE NORTH STAR

In the Northern Hemisphere, the North Star sits directly above the geographic North Pole. But to find it, you first need to locate a constellation (group of stars) called the Big Dipper.

Draw an imaginary line straight up from the lowest two stars until your reach the next bright star. This is the North Star. It is the last star in the 'handle' of the Little Dipper constellation.

North Star

...rth Star forms
...d of the tail
...ittle Dipper
...llation.

Follow the end of the Big Dipper up to locate the North Star.

...Big Dipper is
...e of the most
...recognisable
...nstellations.

TOP TIPS

By calculating how high the North Star is above the horizon, it is possible to work out your latitude. Sailors have been using this method to guide them on their travels since ancient times.

To help you navigate accurately when you're out in the countryside, it's useful to know how far you've travelled from your last point. If you have a map with a scale or access to GPS, it's easy. But what if you don't?

PACING

You can estimate how far you've walked by counting your steps.

Place a tape measure on the ground. Then, starting with your right foot, walk forward two steps.

Measure the distance you walked and round it up or down to the nearest half metre. Make sure you walk normally – don't take a giant stride.

When out walking, count how many times you step off from your right foot. Then multiply that number by your stride distance and you'll have an idea of how far you've travelled.

Count your steps as you walk to avoid becoming lost.

TOP TIPS

Measure your steps walking on flat ground, then going uphill, then going downhill. Make sure you use the figure that is the most appropriate for your terrain.

TIMING

Another way of estimating your distance is to use a technique called timing.

Time yourself walking at a steady pace over a measured distance, such as 1 km.

When you are out in the countryside, note the time it takes you to walk between two set points. From that, you can calculate the approximate distance that you have covered.

Don't forget that your speed will vary from flat ground to hills, and from roads to tall grass.

7:07 15

PLANNING A ROUTE

You know how to read a map. You've learned the Country Code. You've practised how to navigate. So, where are you going to go with these skills? It's time to plan your first route.

Before going on an adventure, it is important to plan your route properly. Your first priority is to make sure your journey will be safe. Your next priority is reaching your destination as quickly and easily as possible.

ROUTE CARDS

To plan a route you will need a map, a compass, a ruler and a route card. On the card, break down your proposed route into separate stages, which you can tick off as you go.

The first bearing is the one that will take you from your start point to your second grid reference.

The first grid reference is where you're going to start.

For each stage, note down the grid reference, bearing, distance and any notes, such as any features you may see or your estimated time. Don't forget to allow for variance or declination.

GRID REFERENCE	BEARING
132546	165°
789112	180°
186986	95°
	45°
	123°
	214°

WARNING ⚠️

Bring an adult

Be sure to take an adult with you on your adventure, so that you stay safe. Also, leave a copy of your route card with someone so that they know where you'll be and can raise the alarm if anything happens.

PLANNING YOUR ROUTE

Make sure you look carefully at the features on your map so that you can build your route around any difficult or possibly dangerous areas, such as steep hills, bogs, rivers and cliffs.

Avoid crossing wide rivers

Finish

Grid reference point

Watch out for steep areas.

By recording the distances between grid references on your route card, you can keep track of where you are during your walk by estimating the distance that you've travelled so far.

DISTANCE	NOTES
1 km	Will see river 1 km from start
3 km	Will see cliffs on left 2 km from start
5 km	Follow the western edge of the lake
7 km	Make a stop at visitor centre
8 km	
10 km	

Writing notes about what you are going to see on each section will also help you to keep on track.

NAME:
ADDRESS:
EMERGENCY CONTACT:
EMERGENCY CONTACT NUMBER:

Your name and address.

Write your contact details on the back of your route card.

A fun way to practise planning a route is to fill out a route card and then test it out as a treasure hunt for your friends.

TREASURE ROUTE

Print a map 1

Print out a map of your local park from the Internet. Or, to make it really fun, you could make a map of your garden (see p.25).

Make a route

Work out a route through your park or garden, and then mark up a route card for orienteering around it.

2

Leave prizes

3

Walk the route on your route card. Every time you get to a new grid reference, leave a prize, such as a badge or a chocolate bar, as well as a number on a sticky note.

Hand out route cards 4

Make versions of the route card and map for your friends and send them off on a treasure hunt. If you've filled out the cards correctly, they should be able to use it to work out where to find the prizes. The quickest orienteer will get the most prizes.

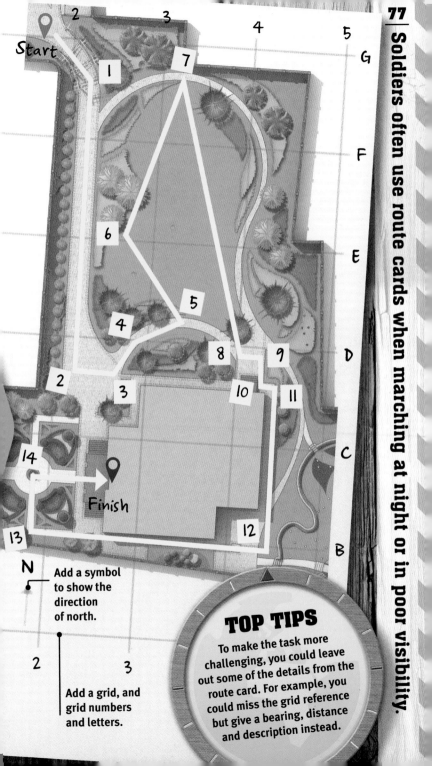

Start

2   3   4   5

G

7

1

F

6

E

5

4   8   9   D

2   3   10   11

C

14

Finish

13   12   B

N
Add a symbol to show the direction of north.

2   3

Add a grid, and grid numbers and letters.

TOP TIPS

To make the task more challenging, you could leave out some of the details from the route card. For example, you could miss the grid reference but give a bearing, distance and description instead.

USING
GPS

Maps have been around for centuries and are still used for outdoor adventures. But modern technology offers some great advantages. Get to grips with GPS to make the most of them.

GPS stands for Global Positioning System. Special GPS satellites orbit the Earth, constantly transmitting a signal that your GPS unit can use to tell where you are anywhere on the planet. Pretty useful!

HOW DOES GPS WORK?

1 A GPS satellite sends out a signal, showing what time it was sent.

2 Your GPS unit receives that signal and compares the time it was sent with the time it was received. It then uses that time difference to calculate how far you are from the satellite.

3 By receiving the time signals from four or more GPS satellites, your GPS unit can use the information to calculate your position to just a few yards. The more signals a GPS unit receives, the more accurate it will be.

Satellite 1

Satellite 2

Satellite 3

Satellite 4

Your position

Distance to each satellite is different

GPS FACTS

There are at least 24 operational GPS satellites orbiting the Earth at any one time, each one following a specific course.

Wherever you are on Earth, you should be able to connect to at least six of them.

They orbit at a height of around 20,200 km above the surface of the Earth, taking 12 hours to go once around the planet.

US scientists realized that GPS was possible in the late 1950s. This was when they began tracking the first satellites by measuring the frequency of their electronic signals. The first GPS satellite was launched in 1978 and the system became fully operational in 1995. It is funded by the US government, but is free for anyone to use.

Launched in 1957 by the Soviet Union, Sputnik 1 was the world's first satellite.

You can plan an entire route on your GPS by entering your destinations into your GPS as 'waypoints'. When you reach each waypoint, your unit will show you which way to travel to get to the next one.

KNOW YOUR GPS

Some GPS units only give your location as a grid reference, while others will show you your position as a marker on a detailed topographic map.

Keep antenna clear

When using GPS, remember to alter the settings to match those of your map – such as the type of grid being displayed and the units used to measure distances (these are usually kilometres or miles).

Your GPS can also tell you lots of other important and useful information about your journey, such as how far you've travelled since your last waypoint, your average speed and how long you have been travelling.

This GPS unit displays lots of information, including your height ('Elevation'), distance walked ('Trip Odometer') and speed.

Sunset in 5 hr 22 min

Elevation
58 m

Trip Odometer
361.4 km

Speed
. kmh

Max Speed
8.3 kmh

Moving time
99:43

Moving Avg
3.6 kmh

Stopped Time
98:44

Overall Avg
1.8 kmh

MOBILE NAVIGATION

Modern smartphones can use GPS signals to locate your position and follow a route on a map. But be aware that they can only be used in places where you can receive a mobile phone signal. Dedicated GPS units can be used anywhere.

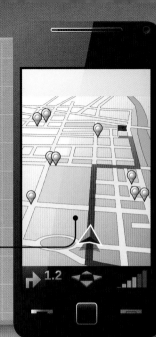

GPS apps on mobile phones have made made navigating much simpler.

GPS units can guide you through remote wildernesses.

WARNING

Don't forget!

⚠ Remember, your GPS relies on batteries, which can run out, so always carry spares.

⚠ GPS receivers can also malfunction, so make sure you practise your navigation skills so you can still find your way with a map and a compass.

A little like an electronic version of orienteering, geocaching is a great way to improve your navigating skills with a GPS unit.

Geocaches have been hidden in some very remote locations.

WHAT IS GEOCACHING?

Invented in 2000, geocaching is a fun outdoor game that you can play with a handheld GPS unit. The aim is to find a hidden container, called a geocache, using waypoints listed on a geocaching website.

Each container contains a logbook and pencil. When you get to the hidden geocache, you sign the book to prove you've been there, then put it back exactly as you found it, so other geocachers can use it.

Most caches also contain 'treasures', such as badges, CDs or books. You can take these, as long as you leave replacements.

A geocache with pencil, logbook and a selection of toys.

TOP TIP

Create your very own geocache by hiding a logbook and pen in a waterproof container, then entering its coordinates onto the geocaching website listed in the back of this book.

FIND IT WITH FRIENDS

You can play your own geocaching racing game, known as 'geodashing', with your friends in your local park.

1 Hide paper, pencils and 'treasure' objects, such as chocolate bars or small toys, in plastic containers around the park.

2 Mark the position of each one as a waypoint on your GPS unit.

3 Make a list of the waypoints as grid references, and give copies to your friends, who should all be equipped with either a GPS unit or a mobile phone.

4 Your friends must then race to track down the treasures using the waypoints, write down their names to prove they've found the caches, and claim their treasures.

Small plastic containers and glass jars make good, secure geocaches. ———

● GEOCACHE DO NOT REMOVE

YOUR FIRST EXPEDITION

You've learned, you've practised, you've planned. Now all that's left is to pull all your mapping skills together and embark on your very own expedition. Where will it take you?

The first stage of your adventure is to carefully plan it. Time spent planning will not only ensure that it's successful and safe, but will also help you to get as much fun out of your adventure as possible.

QUESTIONS AND ANSWERS

To get you thinking about your adventure in more detail, try coming up with answers to some of the following questions:

Where are you going?
The local park • Out into the countryside • Up into the hills • Down to the coast

How will you get there?
Walk • Bus • Train • Car

What are you planning to do when you get there?
Visit landmarks • Take photographs • Look for flowers • Go bird-watching

How long will you be going for?
A few hours • An overnight trip • Several days

Who else will be going on the adventure with you?
Friends • Siblings • Adults

WHAT ROUTE?

Now that you know how to read a map and plan a route, it's time to put those skills into practice and and create a route card for your first adventure.

Look at your map carefully when planning the adventure to make sure you choose the easiest, safest route possible.

Even if you're going to use a GPS unit to guide you, fill out a route card as well, just in case your GPS fails.

TOP TIPS

• Always make sure you have permission from your parents and the owners of the land before setting off.

• Your first adventure doesn't have to be a walk. You could go for a long bike ride.

WARNING

Stay Safe!

Never head out on a mapping adventure unless there's an adult who can come with you.

What equipment you bring will depend on where you are going, what the weather will be like and how long you are going for. Make an equipment checklist, lay out all your equipment and practise packing.

EQUIPMENT CHECKLIST

NAVIGATION EQUIPMENT:

Map

GPS unit

Compass

Route card

Pencil and paper

Binoculars

EQUIPMENT TO KEEP YOU SAFE:

Spare batteries for GPS unit

Mobile phone

Penknife – be sure to get the help of an adult before using

Foil blanket

First aid kit

Whistle

Watch

FOOD AND DRINK:

Meals and snacks

Bottle of water

PACK CAREFULLY

Never leave packing to the last minute. You need to know that you can fit everything you require in your bag and that you can carry it easily.

Pack in layers with the least important things at the bottom and the essentials at the top. Put anything you'll be using regularly, such as a map, a compass or your mobile phone, into easy-to-access outside pockets.

WALKING GEAR:

Walking boots or shoes

Waterproof clothes

Day pack or rucksack

OVERNIGHT GEAR:

Tent

Sleeping bag and mat

Cooking stove and matches – use only under close adult supervision

Wind-up torch

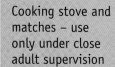

With your route planned and your bag packed, it's time to put your new mapping and navigation skills to the test. Have fun and remember to stay safe!

Bearing the direction from your current position to your destination, as measured in degrees on a compass.

Cartography making maps – a cartographer is a map-maker.

Compass rose a symbol on a map showing the compass points.

Contour a line on a map that links areas of the same height.

Degrees units used to divide up circles, such as a compass dial, and spheres, such as a globe.

Equator an imaginary line running horizontally around the centre of the Earth, marking the line of 0° latitude.

Globe a spherical (ball-shaped) representation of the Earth.

GPS stands for Global Positioning System, a method for locating positions on the planet using a GPS unit and a network of satellites.

Grid a series of intersecting lines overlaying a map and dividing it into equal-sized boxes, which can be used for pinpointing locations.

Grid references a code made up of numbers, or letters and numbers, which can be used to find a location on a map using its grid.

Hemisphere half the Earth – the Equator divides the Earth into Northern and Southern Hemispheres.

Latitude a way of measuring something's position north or south of the Equator using a series of imaginary lines running horizontally around the Earth.

Legend the map's key, which tells you what the scale is, the direction of north and what the symbols and colours mean.

Longitude a way of measuring something's position east or west of the Prime Meridian using a series of imaginary lines called lines of longitude.

Map a picture or a diagram showing an area of land as if it were being seen from above.

Navigate to plan a route, or to travel along a planned route.

Orient to use a compass to line up something – such as a map – in the right direction.

Orienteering a sport in which competitors use a map and a compass to guides themselves around a course.

Prime Meridian the line of 0° longitude, running vertically around the Earth from which all locations east or west are measured.

Route card a card on which a route has been planned out in detail.

Satellite a spacecraft placed in orbit around the planet, which sends information back down to receivers on Earth.

Scale the amount by which an area of land has been shrunk down to fit on a map.

Scale bar a symbol on a map showing what scale has been used.

Topographic a type of map that shows a small area in great detail and highlights the height of land using contour lines.

Variance the difference between the direction of True North, Magnetic North and Grid North which must be accounted for when planning a route.

Waypoint a grid reference, or set of coordinates, which can be used to identify a particular place or landmark.

earthobservatory.nasa. gov/GlobalMaps/ Look through an assortment of themed global maps from the U.S. space agency NASA, including ones showing the distribution of vegetation, snow cover, and rainfall patterns. The earthobservatory.nasa.gov site is packed with dazzling satellite images of the Earth.

www.geocaching.com/ play Find out about the global treasure hunt known as geocaching and join in yourself.

www.google.co.uk/intl/ en_uk/earth/ Use Google's up-to-the-minute technology to virtually explore the entire planet (including undersea terrains), take 3-D fly pasts of cities, browse historic maps, and even examine maps of the Moon and Mars.

www.google.co.uk/maps Zoom in and out of maps, 3-D pictures and satellite images from right across the world, and plan detailed routes.

maps.nationalgeographic. com/maps Explore a wide range of themed maps at this National Geographic site.

www.rmg.co.uk/national- maritime-museum Find out more about the history of navigation at the National Maritime Museum in Greenwich, UK, the home of the Prime Meridian.

www.rgs.org/HomePage. htm Discover the world of maps at Britain's Royal Geographical Society, which holds one of the largest private map and chart collections in the world.

www.ordnancesurvey.co. uk/docs/leaflets/map- reading-made-easy- peasy.pdf Let Ordnance Survey, Britain's premier map-making organisation, teach you some of the basics of map reading.

About the Author

Justin Miles is a British professional adventurer and has honed his mapping and navigation skills in some of the more extreme areas of the world. His adventures include exploring the Arctic, climbing mountains, exploring deserts and hacking his way through jungles. All of Justin's experiences have been used to support charities and to fuel various education projects.

Justin turned his passion for adventure into his profession after a car accident in 1999 resulted in brain injuries that left him having to learn to walk and talk again from scratch. It was during his recovery that he decided he would become a 'full-time' explorer and use his experiences to support charities and inspire children to learn through innovative education programmes. Justin is a passionate supporter of the global education programme 'Educate A Child'.

Acknowledgements

The publisher thanks the following agencies for their kind permission to use their images.

Key: t=top, b=bottom, l=left, r=right

Alamy
11bl © North Wind Picture Archives , 11br © iPhone

Dreamstime
3br © Gawriloff, 13b © Steven Huff, 24br © Kenliu, 51tr © Timothy Epp, 88c © Kenliu

iStock.com
1 © malerapaso, 4–5 © bravobravo, 5 © TommL, 6–7 © tzahiV, 12–13 © baldas1950, 16–17 © pixproviderAB, 17bl © Edin, 18–19 © incombile, 20–21 © alarich, 24cr © Poligrafistka, 24cl © Jonathan Woodcock, 25tr © tomeng, 25r © Jia He, 26–27 © incombile, 28–29 © Neonci, 30–31 © agustavop, 30bl © soberve, 32–33 © AdrianHillman, 32c © xalanx, 32bc © Young777, 33t © Adventure_Photo, 38–39 © Csondy, 40–41 © quintanilla, 40bl © Juanmonino, 40br © leezsnow, 41tr cunfek, 42–43 © EasyBuy4u, 42cl © -art-siberia-, 43br © Neonci, 44–45 © kodachrome25, 44b © Boyloso, 45br © ellend1022, 46–47 © JacquiMD, 48–49 © dvoevnore, 48bl © HadelProductions, 49br © cristimateï, 50–51 © emregologlu, 51tl © THPStock, 51cl © AKS_Photo, 51cr © alexandrumagurean, 51bl © pialhovik, 51be © evergreenpics, 52c © serggn, 54–55 © javarman3, 56–58 © toddarbini, 57br © kickstand, 58–59 © DNY59, 60–61 © Wildroze, 61tr © stocksnapper, 61br © JulieanneBirch, 62–62 © Khrizmo, 62c © gemenacom, 62bl © Extropy, 63br © IPGGutenbergUKLtd, 64–65 © JLGutierrez,

66–67 © Marek Mnich, 67br © tioloco, 68–69 © angelinast, 70–71 © angelinast, 70bl © lmsvail99, 71br © Prykhodov, 72–73 © hkeita, 74–75 © Jonathan Woodcock, 77 © ThreeDiCube, 78–79 © M_a_y_a, 81t © BlackJack3D, 81br © EduardHarkonen, 82–83 © mel-nik, 82bl © SanderStock, 83tr © oh_design, 84–85 © ra-photos, 85br © Lasse_Hendriks, 86–87 © Kemter, 88tr © Gyrohype, 89b © Erik Khalitov, 91tr © nbehmans, 94tl © BlackJack3D, 95br © HadelProductions, 95bl © Extropy

NASA
24–25 © NASA

NOAA
36–37 © Submarine Ring of Fire 2014 - Ironman, NOAA/PMEL, NSF, 50cl © NOAA's Office of Coast Survey Historical Map and Chart Collection

Shutterstock.com
2br © djgis, 3tl © zlikovec, 2–3 © Kvadrat, 8cr © AridOcean, 8cl © Johanna Goodyear, 8br © Thinglass, 9tl © PGMart, 9b © djgis, 10–11 © Rainer Lesniewski, 10cr © Ioannis Ioannou, 10b © RTimages, 11tl © ekler, 13tr © cetus, 14–15 © PeterPhoto123, 14br © Glowonconcept, 15tr © Martina Vaculikova, 15bl © Pablo Scapinachis, 23br © Seamartini Graphics, 31tl © Bardocz Peter, 59tr & 63 cr © StockPhotosArt, 75tr © Robert Adrian Hillman, 76–77, 88–89 & 90–91 © PeterPhoto123, 93br © Pablo Scapinachis, 92–93 & 94–95 © Rainer Lesniewski, 95c © djgis

Public Domain
50tc Daderot

Other
49tr © PHGCOM, 84bl © i_am_jim